Journal Your Life's Journey

A Blank Book Billionaire Creation

52217649R00059

Made in the USA
San Bernardino, CA
19 August 2017